CONTENTS

SCHOOL FOR DRAGONS
By Ann Jungman

ABOUT THE SERIES
INSIDE FRONT COVER

BACKGROUND INFORMATION
3-5

LESSON PLANS
6-19

WHAT IS A DRAGON?	6
WHAT DOES THE BOOK COVER TELL US?	7
WHY DO WE READ?	8
DRAGONS CAN BE FUNNY!	9
LET'S WRITE A PLAY!	10
SCHOOL LIFE	12
FIRST DAYS AT SCHOOL	13
LET'S WRITE A POEM	14
THE STORY OF SAINT GEORGE AND THE DRAGON	15
WRITING MI'S SCHOOL REPORT	16
CHARACTERS IN THE BOOK	17
FIRE DRILL	18
BOOK REVIEW	19

PHOTOCOPIABLES
20-32

DESCRIBING DRAGONS!	20
WHAT WILL HAPPEN?	21
BRAINSTORM	22
WRITING A DIALOGUE	23
LET'S WRITE A PLAY!	24
WHAT DO THESE WORDS MEAN?	25
THE DIARY OF MI	26
FIRE POEM	27
ST GEORGE AND THE DRAGONS	28
SCHOOL REPORT	29
CHARACTER WORK – MRS JEFFRIES AND MI	30
FIRE! FIRE!	31
BOOK REVIEW	32

SKILLS GRID
INSIDE BACK COVER

CREDITS

Published by Scholastic Ltd,
Villiers House,
Clarendon Avenue,
Leamington Spa,
Warwickshire CV32 5PR
Text © Kate Caton
© 1998 Scholastic Ltd
1 2 3 4 5 6 7 8 9 0   8 9 0 1 2 3 4 5 6 7

Author Kate Caton
Series consultant Fiona Collins
Editor Jane Bishop
Series designer Lynne Joesbury
Designer Lynne Joesbury
Illustrations John Eastwood
Cover illustration John Eastwood

Designed using Adobe Pagemaker

British Library Cataloguing-in-Publication Data
A catalogue record for this book is available from the British Library.

ISBN 0-590-63648-0

The right of Kate Caton to be identified as the Author of this work has been asserted by her in accordance with the Copyright, Designs and Patents Act 1988.

All rights reserved. This book is sold subject to the condition that it shall not, by way of trade or otherwise, be lent, hired out or otherwise circulated without the publisher's prior consent in any form of binding or cover other than that in which it is published and without a similar condition, including this condition, being imposed upon the subsequent purchaser.

No part of this publication may be reproduced, stored in a retrieval system, or transmitted, in any form or by any means, electronic, mechanical, photocopying, recording or otherwise, without the prior permission of the publisher. This book remains copyright, although permission is granted to copy pages 20 to 32 for classroom distribution and use only in the school which has purchased the book and in accordance with the CLA licensing agreement. Photocopying permission is given for purchasers only and not for borrowers of books from any lending service.

ACKNOWLEDGEMENTS

Bloomsbury Publishing Plc for text taken from the book *Harry Potter and the Philosopher's Stone* by JK Rowling © 1997, JK Rowling (1997, Bloomsbury Publishing Plc)
Oxford University Press for the use of text from *Saint George and the Dragon* by Geraldine McCaughrean © 1989, Geraldine McCaughrean (1989, Oxford University Press)
Every effort has been made to trace copyright holders and the publishers apologise for any inadvertent omissions.

BACKGROUND INFORMATION

GENRE

School For Dragons is a story divided into six chapters with illustrations, set in the present day in a junior school. The combination of realistic characters and dragons brings a part-believable, part-fantastic nature to the story. Children will find the school setting familiar and all the characters in the story are likeable, each with a sense of humour. Readers will warm instantly to the main character, M1 the little dragon who wants to learn to read, and will eagerly follow him through his first weeks at Merringham Junior School, enjoying the string of activities in which he gets involved.

PLOT SUMMARY

The story opens with a fire at the school, which has been started by a small dragon called M1 who is intent on learning to read. Three of the school children befriend M1 and read stories to him. M1 is eventually admitted to the school as a pupil despite his parents' reservations. He is welcomed by staff and pupils alike and shows himself to be a first-class pupil. When excited he does tend to breathe fire which gives rise to some worrying incidents! However, he also uses his fire breathing to good effect, as a stimulus for poetry writing, in science and drama lessons. When his parents realise the value of M1's education, they are persuaded to allow their other dragon children to join the school, making Merringham Junior School truly a 'School For Dragons'.

ABOUT THE AUTHOR

Ann Jungman grew up in North London and had a very ordinary childhood; there were certainly no signs of any interest in or ability at writing. At Exeter University, she studied law and then read for the Bar. While studying, she did some supply teaching which seemed much more fun and challenging than law, so Ann trained to be a primary school teacher! Ann says that the best part of teaching was reading books with the children.

She began to invent her own stories, which the children liked, and they encouraged her to write them down. After some years one was published, *Fang and the Fiery Dragon*. After that she had a number of short books published and then, after visiting Transylvania – vampire country – her character *Vlad* was born. In order to make him seem harmless, Ann decided to make him a vegetarian! It took seven years to find a publisher for this book; no one thought books about vampires were suitable for children. However, once published, *Vlad* was a big success and Ann wrote six more books about him. Ann has also written about wolves, bandits, dragons, more vampires, trolls, witches and ghosts. Her books range from picture books up to 50,000 word novels and cover an age range of three to 13. Since giving up teaching, Ann has spent most of her time writing stories, but has also done some adult teaching and research for television.

In addition to the eighty five books that Ann has written, she has also had a play, 'Marco Polo' performed, had many stories read on radio and seven of her books have been read on television.

Ann lives in London, after five wonderful years in Australia, and, apart from travel, she loves to read, walk, cook, talk and go to the theatre, opera, ballet, cinema and galleries and reluctantly admits to watching too much television.

BACKGROUND INFORMATION

ABOUT THE ILLUSTRATOR

John Eastwood has written and illustrated a wide variety of books for children, including another one about dragons – *Puddletown Dragon* (Young Piper series).

SPECIFIC TEACHING OPPORTUNITIES

TEXT LEVEL

School For Dragons provides many opportunities to introduce children to other literature with links to this story or similar themes. These opportunities include the traditional story of Saint George and the Dragon, *Harry Potter and the Philosopher's Stone* (JK Rowling), *The Last of the Dragons* (E Nesbit), *The Lion, the Witch and the Wardrobe* (CS Lewis), *The Hobbit* (Tolkein), other poetry about dragons and other stories set in schools (see listing on page 5).

The main character in *School For Dragons* is desperate to learn to read and this provides an excellent starting point for a discussion about why and how we read. One lesson plan (page 7) asks the children to predict the general storyline of the book using chapter titles and illustrations as clues.

The book is rich in dialogue and provides opportunities for the children to role-play and become involved in writing a playscript. Other events and ideas in the story can be used for creative writing in different genres, including diary writing, poetry and procedural writing.

Other text-level elements explored are the identification of humour in the story, skimming and scanning for specific information, summarizing key events, characterisation and reviewing the book.

SENTENCE LEVEL

A range of sentence level work can be derived from the story. As the central character is a dragon, one of the children's first tasks is to write their own definition of such a creature. They also look closely at the book cover, making inferences from the blurb.

There is an abundance of dialogue in the story, providing opportunities for the children to identify direct speech and look at punctuation in dialogue, while the study of characterization through the text prompts the children's own character descriptions and creating the dragon's school report demands brevity in the children's writing. Lesson plans also focus on cloze procedure, précis work, summarizing and writing instructions.

WORD LEVEL

Work at word level includes investigating new vocabulary, on the dragon theme, using dictionaries and exploring spelling patterns (-tle, -gle, -ble, -ing) using words from the text. The theme of fire, which plays a major part in the story, is used as a stimulus for some of the word-level activities, looking at the use of adjectives and verbs, and also choosing adjectives to describe variations in colour.

Lesson plans also focus on developing book language (such as spine, blurb), synonyms for 'said' and similes.

THE ACTIVITIES

The book is written in six chapters and lesson plans focus on each chapter in turn, one lesson plan for each of Chapters 1, 2, 3 and 6, and two lesson plans for Chapters 4 and 5.

In addition, the first two lesson plans contain 'Before reading' activities, while the last three lesson plans focus on 'After reading' activities.

BACKGROUND INFORMATION

THE POSTER
SIDE 1

The extracts from *The Last of the Dragons* E Nesbit, *Saint George and the Dragon* Geraldine McCaughrean and *Harry Potter and the Philosopher's Stone* JK Rowling on the poster are to support the first 'Before reading' lesson plan, 'What is a dragon?' on page 6, where the children are introduced to dragons in other literature. The extracts provide an abundance of interesting vocabulary to investigate (wrought, crevices) painting pictures in the imagination to share and discuss together.

SIDE 2

The five extracts from the text in Substituting words are used for vocabulary and dictionary work in the lesson plan for Chapter 4, 'School life' on page 12.

The seven extracts from the text, Learning about characters, are used in the 'After reading' lesson plan, 'Characters in the book' on page 17, to show the children how they can build a character profile by learning about a character from the text.

LINKED RESOURCES
BOOKS WITH A DRAGON THEME

Saint George and the Dragon Geraldine McCaughrean (Oxford University Press)
The Last of the Dragons E Nesbit (Puffin – currently out of print)
Harry Potter and the Philosopher's Stone JK Rowling (Bloomsbury Publishing)
Charlie, Emma and the Dragon Family Margaret Greaves (out of print)
Charlie, Emma and Juggling Dragon Margaret Greaves (out of print)
Charlie's Dragon Lesley Harker (Hamish Hamilton)
Dragonrise Kathryn Cave (Young Puffin)

BOOKS WITH BOTH A DRAGON AND SCHOOL THEME

Dragon in Class 4 June Counsel (Corgi Yearling Books)
Dragon in Top Class June Counsel (Corgi Yearling Books)
Dragon in Summer June Counsel (Corgi Yearling Books)

BOOKS WITH A SCHOOL THEME

Mr Majeika and the School Play Humphrey Carpenter (Young Puffin)
Mr Majeika and the Music Teacher Humphrey Carpenter (Young Puffin)
Mr Majeika and the School Inspector* Humphrey Carpenter (Young Puffin)
Mr Majeika and the School Book Week* Humphrey Carpenter (Young Puffin)
*Also on Cavalcade Story Cassettes

OTHER BOOKS BY ANN JUNGMAN

Lucy and the Big Bad Wolf (Young Lions/Chivers Audio Books)
Lucy and the Wolf in Sheep's Clothing (Young Lions/Chivers Audio Books)
Lucy keeps the Wolf from the Door (Young Lions/Chivers Audio Books)

OTHER BOOKS IN THE *YOUNG HIPPO SCHOOL STORIES* SERIES

Off to School Jean Chapman
The Grott Street Gang Terry Deary
Nightingale News Odette Elliott
Class Four's Wild Week Malcolm Yorke (out of print)
Pet Swapping Day/Whizz Bang and the Crocodile Room Susan Gates

LESSON PLANS

BEFORE READING

WHAT IS A DRAGON?
RESOURCES NEEDED

Poster, one copy of the Oxford English Dictionary, classroom dictionaries for the children, whiteboard/flip chart, rough paper for notes, photocopiable page 20, writing materials. You could also have available books about myths, preferably with pictures of dragons and also books relating to reptiles.

WHOLE-CLASS WORK

Look at the descriptions of dragons on the poster from *The Last of the Dragons* E Nesbit (Puffin – currently out of print), *Saint George and the Dragon* by Geraldine McCaughrean (Oxford University Press) and *Harry Potter and the Philosopher's Stone* by J K Rowling (Bloomsbury Publications).

Read through the first extract from *The Last of the Dragons* with the children. Ask them to describe in their own words the picture they see in their minds. Do they understand all the vocabulary? What do these words mean: vast, scaly, sheen, gleaming? Can they understand the simile 'his silvery sheen gleaming like diamonds in the sun'?

Now read through the extract from *Saint George and the Dragon* and repeat the activity looking at these words and phrases: crevices; a wreath of sinew and claw; gaped; lidless eyes; stretched and withdrew; foul breath.

Finally look at the third piece from *Harry Potter and the Philosopher's Stone* looking at the words: spiny; jet; snout; stubs of horns.

As the title of the book *School for Dragons* suggests, the story revolves around a dragon. An initial discussion of what the children already know about dragons would be a useful way of approaching the story.

Collect together all their ideas and then use the Oxford English Dictionary with the children to look to look up the definition of dragon (mythical monster like reptile, usually with wings and claws and often breathing fire). Help the children use any other dictionaries that you may have in the classroom to find any further descriptive words. Use a board or flip chart to write down any key words which you find from your sources, encouraging the children to remember the words and phrases for you to list.

Discuss the word 'mythical' and help the children use dictionaries to look up a definition. (Mythical, mythology, <u>myth</u> – traditional narrative usually involving supernatural ...). Enlarge on and discuss the definitions, explaining the words used to the children. Again, write down key words on the chart or another page of the flip chart paper.

Go on to discuss the word 'monster' and use dictionaries in the same way to investigate a definition. (Monster – misshapen animal ... imaginary animal compounded of incongruous elements ...). As before, discuss the definitions and make brief notes.

Finally, discuss the word 'reptile' and look up a definition. (Reptile – member of the Reptilia or class of animals including snakes, lizards, crocodiles, turtles and tortoises ...). Discuss the definitions found and use any relevant reference books you have to establish the cold-blooded nature of reptiles and to look at pictures of lizards, particularly 'bearded dragon lizards'. Make some brief notes about what you have found out.

GROUP WORK

The children can work in mixed-ability groups to discuss and record the definitions of the 'dragon' words. Each group should elect a scribe. They can refer to the notes made in the previous session and discuss the two or three sentences they will create from these notes. The scribe should then write these on rough paper

LESSON PLANS

as the children discuss the best ways to phrase and word their ideas. When all members of the group are happy with their sentences, they can be copied neatly by each child onto the photocopiable sheet.

The second task on photocopiable page 20 'Describing dragons' asks the children to pull together the information they have gathered and discussed and to write an explanation of what a dragon is. Each child can then write his or her own individual descriptions on the sheet.

PLENARY

The groups will feedback to the rest of the class, reading out their word-meanings and their dragon definitions. Based on five groups of six children, each group could make two feedback contributions, for example Mythical (two groups), Monster (two groups), Reptile (three groups), Dragon (three groups). Ask the rest of the class to evaluate the findings for clarity, accuracy and language flow. Finish with a fun activity, listening to the song 'Puff the magic dragon' or reading the words as a poem!

WHAT DOES THE BOOK COVER TELL US?

BEFORE READING

RESOURCES NEEDED

Photocopiable page 21, writing materials.

WHOLE-CLASS WORK

Explain to the children that the cover of a book is often designed to give the prospective reader a flavour of what the book is about and what kind of book it is – sad, humorous, serious.

From looking at the front cover, ask the children for their first impressions of the book *School for Dragons*. Ask them to give their reasons for those impressions. Raise the questions: What is the story about? Will it be realistic? Why not? What message do the bright colours give? (Light-hearted rather than serious and gloomy.) Who is the author?

Turn to the back cover with the children and read the blurb with them. (Blurb – brief word 'picture' of contents.) Why do the children think the dragon is called M1? What is his problem? Where is the story set? What other information can be found on the back cover? Identify other book features including the name of the illustrator, publisher, price, ISBN and series name.

Now ask the children to read the first page (before the title page). Why is this one page given at the beginning of the book? Do the children think they'll enjoy the story? Why?

Turn over to the next page and point out the two lists of stories. Discuss why the lists are there and ask the children which book title appeals most to them.

Look at the Hippo logo on the title page and on the spine. Point out that this logo will be found on other Hippo books in schools, libraries and shops and tell the children to look out for it.

As preparation for the group work, look briefly through the book together at each chapter title and the illustrations. This will give the children clues to help them predict what might happen in each chapter. Make brief comments, suggestions about the story and ask questions as you see each picture, to inspire the children's predictions in their group work. For example, in Chapter 1 'The Fire', the illustrations show: a burning book, the teacher reading to the class, the teacher with her whistle and children looking surprised, the school watching the burning building, the fireman hosing the fire, talking to a man (the headteacher?) and holding a small dragon.

LITERACY HOUR UNITS — SCHOOL FOR DRAGONS

LESSON PLANS

GROUP WORK

Split the children into six ability groups and ask the children to predict what might happen in certain chapters, having looked at the chapter titles and illustrations in the whole-class session. The two less able groups could work on Chapters 1 and 2. The next two groups could work on Chapters 5 and 6. The two more able groups could work on Chapters 3 and 4 initially but could carry on into Chapters 5 and 6 if they have time.

Give each child a copy of photocopiable page 21, 'What will happen?'. Read it through with them, making sure they understand what is required. Assure the children that they are not expected to predict exactly what does happen and that there are no right or wrong answers. Explain that you want them to make sensible predictions from the information they have extracted from the chapter titles and the illustrations. This is a good opportunity to stress the importance of illustrations in a story and how they elaborate the text. They often also add great enjoyment to the reading process of course, and you can encourage the children to look at and talk about illustrations in any books they are reading.

PLENARY

Choose one child from each of the six groups to read their prediction for one particular chapter to the other children. Discuss each prediction and allow the other children to briefly compare their prediction for that chapter before moving on to the next chapter prediction.

WHY DO WE READ?

PLOT SUMMARY – CHAPTER 1

DURING READING

In this chapter the children of Class 4J are having a story read to them at the end of a school day. The firebell sounds and the children file outside. The school stockroom is on fire and the school has to be evacuated. Fire engines arrive and spray the stockroom with water. A fireman climbs inside the stockroom and finds the culprit – a small dragon, who is rescued from the burning building. He started the fire!

RESOURCES NEEDED

Selected passage from *School for Dragons* to read to the class, whiteboard or flip chart, photocopiable page 22, writing materials.

WHOLE-CLASS WORK

School for Dragons focuses on M1, the small dragon who is rescued from the burning stockroom. He is desperate to learn to read!

Introduce the theme by talking to the children about what reading is, asking them to explain it to you. Ask the children what we read and when. Make a list on the whiteboard/flip chart with the children of all the times we use reading skills in our daily lives (stories, comics, magazines, newspapers, signposts, menus, computer screens, CD covers and so on). Next, consider why we read. Encourage the children to establish the idea that we read to gather information, follow instruction and as an enjoyable activity that can bring immense pleasure. Distinguish for them between fiction and non-fiction.

Next, consider how we read. Read a short passage from *School for Dragons* without any intonation or

LESSON PLANS

expression. Ask the children to comment on the reading and to give you suggestions for how to improve your reading. Invite a volunteer to re-read the passage with intonation and expression, reflecting the comments and suggestions made by the other children. Ensure the children have also understood how important punctuation is to the reader and therefore its importance when we write.

Refer to pages 6–9 of the *School for Dragons* where there is mention of the book *The Lion, the Witch and the Wardrobe* by CS Lewis (Collins). Who has read the book? What happens? Does the witch kill Aslan? Do you think Mrs Jeffries' class were enjoying the story? Why did they like the story?

Lead on to discuss fire and some associated vocabulary (include adjectives and verbs). Explain that we perceive fire using sight, hearing, smell and feeling (for safety avoid using the word 'touch' in this context). Remind the children of bonfires they have seen or burning buildings on television. Discuss language and vocabulary to do with fire in preparation for the cloze activity the children will do in the group session. Talk about adjectives and verbs and encourage the children to state whether the words they contribute are adjectives or verbs. Refer to the fire passage in the book yourself, to ensure any useful words are included by the children.

GROUP WORK

Give each child a copy of photocopiable page 22 'Brainstorm'. Advise groups of less able children to think of appropriate words and then write some sentences. Groups of more able children can think of appropriate words and then go on to the cloze activity. Any children who successfully complete their allotted two tasks can go on to try the third if there is time. Before they begin, read through the sheet with the children making sure they know what to do.

PLENARY

Ask children from each group to volunteer some of the senses words they have found. Discuss the most popular as well as the most unusual suggestions. Read through the cloze passage, allowing the children who have completed this section to offer their words at each gap.

DRAGONS CAN BE FUNNY!
PLOT SUMMARY – CHAPTER 2

DURING READING

The children wonder what will happen to the little dragon now. Three of the children, Lisa, Jessie and Nelson stay behind to help their teacher, but really they want to know what will happen to the baby dragon. The dragon explains that he was in the stockroom because he wanted to look at the picture books. He admits he cannot read and Lisa, Jessie and Nelson all offer to help him by reading stories to him. He tells them his name is M1 and explains why. The children arrange to read to him after school each day.

RESOURCES NEEDED

Photocopiable page 23, writing materials.

WHOLE-CLASS WORK

Start with a discussion in which you reflect with the children on the nature of 'real' dragons. Invite them to contribute sentences or words to reflect what they know about dragons, for example: fierce, dangerous to people, powerful, living in mountains or forests, mythical creatures from times gone by and so on.

LESSON PLANS

Now read Chapter 2 aloud to the children, asking them to listen out and identify when they hear something in the story which they find funny or incongruous with real dragons, according to your previous discussion. Stop and discuss any points raised. Also stop and discuss points that the children fail to react to. They may not have found the humour or identified the incongruity.

Here are some suggestions for discussion:
Once he'd found his tongue, Mr Wilkinson seemed remarkably calm! Would your headteacher seem as calm? (page 17);
The dragon was sitting on Mrs Jeffries' knee, weeping and speaking! Dragons are usually fierce! (page 24);
The dragon blew his nose on a hankie and wanted to look at picture books! (page 26);
Mr Wilkinson suggested the dragon could have gone to the library. As if that was the most normal thing in the world for a dragon to do! (page 27);
The dragon breathes fire when he's happy and excited – quite the opposite of real dragons. Mr Wilkinson calls him 'young man' by mistake! (page 32).

GROUP WORK

Work with a lower ability group, looking closely at pages 34–38. There is a conversation between the children and M1. Explain that the words spoken in the conversation are called the dialogue. Ask each child to choose a character to play (Lisa, Jessie, Nelson, M1 and the narrator). Two children could share the narrator's part if necessary. Help the children read from page 34 (As they walked...) to the end of the chapter, with each character reading their dialogue and the narrator(s) reading the narrative. Ask the individual characters to notice whether their dialogue is simply stated or if it is cried, chimed, called or even said with a smile!

This activity gives children the experience of reading dialogue and taking notice of the punctuation. They will distinguish between dialogue and narrative and learn how important it is to use proper punctuation when writing both forms.

Children in the remaining groups can each have a copy of photocopiable page 23, 'Writing dialogue' to work on punctuating five sentences, distinguishing between the dialogue and the narrative. The second activity on the page focuses on using words other than 'said'.

PLENARY

Ask the group that role-played pages 34–38 to perform to the rest of the class.

For a final short activity, to demonstrate how much more interesting writing can be when different words are used, the children, working individually or in groups, may like to dramatize the last five sentences they worked on, for example whispering 'What do you think is going to happen to the dragon?'

LET'S WRITE A PLAY!
PLOT SUMMARY – CHAPTER 3

DURING READING

M1 joins the children for his first story session, and then comes to meet them every day at 4pm. Mrs Jeffries says he should learn to read for himself, and should come to school! M1's father visits Mrs Jeffries to discuss this. The children explain what a great help M1 could be at home, if he could read to his younger brothers and sisters, and eventually Mr Dragon agrees.

LESSON PLANS

RESOURCES NEEDED

Photocopiable page 24, writing materials, writing guidelines, spare sheets of A4 paper, scissors, glue.

WHOLE-CLASS WORK

Invite some of the children to act out the story, between pages 47 and 55. Help them to decide how many characters there are (there are seven: narrator, Mrs Jeffries, Lisa, Jessie, Nelson, M1 and Mr Dragon). Act it out the first time with one group of children, guiding them with helpful comments as they read their parts (for example, on page 47 – it is not necessary to include 'declared Mrs Jeffries'). The children will read their parts from copies of the book.

Play the scene a second time with a different group of children who will probably give a more fluent 'performance' having learned from watching and listening to the first group. You could even suggest that they characterize their voices.

Discuss with the children whether it would be simpler to read the story as a play if it were written out as a playscript. Ask them to suggest ways of doing this. Remind them of playscripts they have read. How were they set out and arranged on the page?

GROUP WORK

Having talked about writing playscripts, the children should be fairly confident about working on a playscript themselves. For the more able groups, give each child photocopiable page 24, 'Let's write a play!' and read through it with them, making sure they understand the page. Ideally, they should work in pairs as there will be much valuable discussion and exchange of ideas as they make decisions with each other, although they could work individually. Provide spare sheets of A4 paper for the children to continue their script on a second piece of paper. Provide writing guidelines for the children to use underneath these subsequent pages.

For the less able groups, give each child a character name and a piece of A4 paper. Each child can then write the pieces of dialogue for that character on the paper, preceded by the character name for each piece. Collect these together, cut them into strips and paste them with all the other dialogue in the correct order onto a new page to form the script. If there are six children in a group, one child could write for both Nelson and Jessie (four pieces of dialogue in total). The other parts in order of size from largest to smallest are narrator and Mrs Jeffries (seven each), Mr Dragon (five), M1 (four) and Lisa (three).

PLENARY

If possible, have at least two more readings of the scene so that everyone has the opportunity to act out the scene and the children can judge whether it is easier to read the play as a playscript. Discuss the merits of a playscript layout compared with the original book, using words such as clarity.

LESSON PLANS

DURING READING

SCHOOL LIFE
PLOT SUMMARY – CHAPTER 4

Chapter 4 welcomes M1 to Merringham Junior School and takes us through his first few weeks as he learns about life at school. The headteacher explains that extra fire extinguishers have been installed, in case of further fires from M1, who says he only blows flames when he gets too excited! There are a few near misses, but M1 avoids setting fire to the school again.

RESOURCES NEEDED

Poster, dictionaries, photocopiable page 25, writing materials, large sheet of card for word list.

WHOLE-CLASS WORK

Ask the children to compare and contrast M1's school with their own school. What is the same? What is different? Points for discussion could include:

* wearing uniform;
* whistle used for start of school (or bell/handsignal from teacher);
* assembly (is it daily?/whole school?/how long?/taken by headteacher?);
* introduction of new pupils (how is this done in your school?);
* fire extinguishers/fire drills;
* seating arrangements in classroom;
* gold stars for good work;
* skipping and other playground games;
* playground supervision;
* staff meetings;
* school inspection.

Ask the children what other school stories they know. Discuss these stories and how the school day and routines in these compare or contrast with M1's school and their own school.

There are many words in *School for Dragons* that may not be familiar to the children and so may prevent them from thoroughly understanding what is written.

Read the extracts in Substituting words on the poster and ask the children for suggestions of words or phrases that could be used instead of (use and explain the term 'substituted for') the highlighted words. Then help the children look for the highlighted words in dictionaries and discuss what they find, making sure they understand the use of abbreviations, italics, numbers and so on in the dictionary. Some words will have more than one meaning given. Which is the appropriate meaning to use? Ask the children to consider the text and choose which word or phrase they will use to replace the highlighted word. Repeat the exercise with the other four extracts.

GROUP WORK

Read through photocopiable page 25, 'What do those words mean?' with the children and explain what they have to do. The first activity gives the children five words. They need to choose and circle one of three words/phrases that means the same as the given word.

The second activity gives five sentences. Each sentence needs to have one of the five words in the first activity substituted for a phrase, which is underlined, in the sentence. The less able group(s) may not get on to this activity.

PLENARY

Discuss with the children how many of them have learned about new words and increased their vocabulary in this session. Talk about the value of learning new

SCHOOL FOR DRAGONS   LITERACY HOUR UNITS

LESSON PLANS

words and perhaps suggest the children make a simple 'New words' list. Pin this up on a classroom wall and encourage the children to write new words they come across from day to day, together with their meanings on the list. This will help promote an interest in learning about new words among the children.

DURING READING

FIRST DAYS AT SCHOOL
RESOURCES NEEDED
Whiteboard or flip chart, appropriate pens, photocopiable page 26, writing materials.

WHOLE-CLASS WORK
Read Chapter 4 up to page 70 and ask the children to help you make a list of the things that happened to M1 on his first day at school:
* Lisa, Nelson and Jessie welcomed him;
* he stood with Mr Wilkinson in assembly;
* all the children agreed to help him;
* he told the school about his family;
* he painted a picture and got excited.

Read on to the end of the chapter and make a further list of what happened in the following weeks:
* he learned to read incredibly fast;
* he got excited when skipping and started a fire;
* he won prizes for good work;
* an inspector is due to visit – is M1 to be hidden?

Ask the children to look at page 58 and find the third paragraph. Read it to them and point out the word 'whistle'. Write this word on the board. Then help them find 'little' on page 68, 'giggled' on page 69, 'incredibly' on page 70, (talk about 'incredible'), 'wibble wobble' on page 73 and 'mumbled' on page 76. Add these words to 'whistle' on the board.

Discuss these words with the children and ask them to spot any similarity in the spelling, such as -le, -tle, -gle and -ble. Invite the children to add any other -le words to the list.

GROUP WORK
Give the children a copy of photocopiable page 26, 'The diary of M1'. Remind them of the two lists of events in M1's first weeks at school that you have made together. Read through the sheet, making sure the children understand what to do. Talk to the children about the abbreviated form of writing that is often used in a personal diary, for example 'Got up' rather than the full sentence, 'I got up this morning'.

All the groups should do the first activity on the photocopiable sheet about 'Day 1'. Those who are able should then continue with 'A few weeks later'.

PLENARY
Let one or two children read their diary entries to the rest of the class. Talk to the children about keeping a diary; a record of one's life serving as a reminder of days past. Mention the famous diaries of Samuel Pepys and Anne Frank. Encourage the children to each buy an exercise book and to start writing their own diary today!

LESSON PLANS

DURING READING

LET'S WRITE A POEM!
PLOT SUMMARY – CHAPTER 5

Chapter 5 tells us about an inspector visiting the school. She is very concerned about a dragon being in the school but comes to realize that he is a great educational asset. One of the lessons she watches is a poetry writing lesson in which M1 provides a real-life stimulus for the children's ideas. On another occasion, she sees him taking part in a play about Saint George and the Dragon.

RESOURCES NEEDED
Photocopiable page 27, writing materials, poster.

WHOLE-CLASS WORK

One of the lessons the inspector watches is a poetry writing session. Read to page 93, then re-read pages 85–90 to the children, returning to M1's poem (page 89) and reading it once again, emphasizing the rhythm or metre. Point out this rhythm and look at the rhymes – flames/aims, do/blue. What other words might rhyme with flame or blue? (Blame, came, fame, game, name/you, who, to, too, two, clue, drew.)

Next, talk about the way the colours are described on page 85 and discuss the meaning of the words used:
* imperial – of an emperor/majestic/magnificent;
* luminous – full of light/bright/shining;
* brilliant – bright/sparkling/striking.

Encourage the children to think of some words they could use to describe colours. Suggest some colours, for example scarlet, purple, orange, blue and yellow. They may contribute, brightest scarlet, regal purple, flaming orange, royal blue and shining yellow.

Next, talk about similes which use colour such as 'as red as a tomato', 'as purple as grapes', 'as orange as an orange' and 'as yellow as the sun'.
Read aloud the descriptions of the flames moving on page 85. Can the children explain or describe what darting, flickering, shimmering and sparkling mean?

Talk about the descriptions of the smoke on pages 87 and 88 and talk about the meaning of drifting (moving slowly on a current of air) and wafting (moving smoothly and lightly through the air). Explain that in these six -ing words, the suffix -ing is added to a root word which is always a verb. Identify the root words (drift/waft/dart/flicker/shimmer/sparkle). Ask which one has had to change when -ing was added. (Sparkle lost the 'e'.) Talk about losing the 'e' before adding -ing (bubble/bubbling) and talk about doubling the consonant after a short vowel sound (tap/tapping).

GROUP WORK

Give each child a copy of photocopiable page 27, 'Fire poem', which ask them to re-read M1's poem on page 89 and then write their own poem based on it, using the same pattern of rhyme and the same rhythm/metre. For example:

*Flames leap high
Into the sky,
Yellow and red
Bright overhead.*

The more able children who finish their poem can work on the second activity adding -ing to root words and then writing sentences.

SCHOOL FOR DRAGONS — LITERACY HOUR UNITS

LESSON PLANS

PLENARY

Ask the children to share their poems with the class. Comment on rhyme and rhythm used. Purely for enjoyment, return to the two poems on the poster and share these with the children. Ask for volunteers from the class to read the poems aloud, emphasizing the humour.

THE STORY OF SAINT GEORGE AND THE DRAGON

RESOURCES NEEDED

Copies of photocopiable page 28, the book *Saint George and the Dragon* by Geraldine McCaughrean (Oxford University Press) – optional. Sheet of A4 paper divided up into six segments – photocopy to provide one per child, flip chart, display board, pins or tacker to display finished work, paper, pencils, crayons.

WHOLE-CLASS WORK

Read pages 94–101 in Chapter 5 about the children performing the play of Saint George and the Dragon.

Hand out photocopiable page 28 'Saint George and the Dragon' and read the story to the children. If you have the book available look at *Saint George and the Dragon* by Geraldine McCaughrean, showing the illustrations on each page to the children. Tell the children what we know about Saint George and explain that there are many myths about him. Make reference to him as Patron Saint of England and the flag of Saint George as part of the Union Flag.

Discuss the different versions of the same story with the children, comparing and contrasting the language used. Ask the children to identify the various adjectives (terrible, futile, heavy and so on) used in the photocopied story and write their suggestions down on the flip chart.

Let the children comment on which parts of the story (either version) they enjoyed most or found most interesting. Can they explain why? Had they heard the story before?

Re-read the story on the photocopiable page to the children and talk about the main events of the storyline as told in this version of the story.

Help the children summarize the story into six parts:
1 Dragon appears – the dragon is seen in the marshes near the city.
2 Sheep – two sheep are fed to the dragon every day.
3 Princess – Cleolinda's name is drawn from the urn.
4 Dragon attacks – the dragon licks its lips and moves towards Cleolinda.
5 Fight – Saint George appears, fights the dragon and rescues Cleolinda.
6 Saint George leaves – he gives his reward money to the Church and the poor and leaves town, never returning.

GROUP WORK

Give each child a copy of the photocopiable sheet and ask them to read through the story again. Hand out the sheets of A4 paper (divided into six segments). Ask the children to draw pictures and write appropriate captions to tell the story of Saint George, using the six main points which you have identified together.

PLENARY

Talk to the children about how different authors write different versions of the same story. Display the children's work (a working display – quickly pinned up so that the children can see each other's work) and let the children look at each other's pictorial versions of the story. Invite comments on the different illustrations and captions.

LITERACY HOUR UNITS — SCHOOL FOR DRAGONS

LESSON PLANS

DURING READING

WRITING M1'S SCHOOL REPORT
PLOT SUMMARY – CHAPTER 6

The school put on a nativity play, for which M1 is the narrator. As plans for the play progress, M1 also assumes the role of a fire, around which the shepherds warm themselves! On the night of the play, M1's parents, brothers and sisters join the other parents to watch the play. The children take matters into their own hands and introduce some new ideas into the play, which is a resounding success. The headteacher meets the Dragon family and tells the younger members he would be happy to have them join the school too.

RESOURCES NEEDED
Photocopiable page 29, writing materials, rough paper.

WHOLE-CLASS WORK

When M1 first joined the school, no one was very sure how he would fit in. As we read through the story we learn how M1 contributed to the school and fitted in very well. Discuss with the children the different ways in which M1 joined in with all the lessons and activities.

Here are some references to help the discussion:
page 71 – hardworking, enthusiastic, helpful and polite;
page 76 – won prizes for good work;
page 82 – very best pupil;
page 85 – breathed fire to help children write poems about fire;
pages 91–92 – heat and uses of fire;
page 93 – boiling water, testing temperature and burning paper;
page 100 – play about Saint George;
page 102 – delightful and enthusiastic;
page 108 – narrator for nativity play;
page 109 – fire for shepherds;
page 118 – fire in stable.

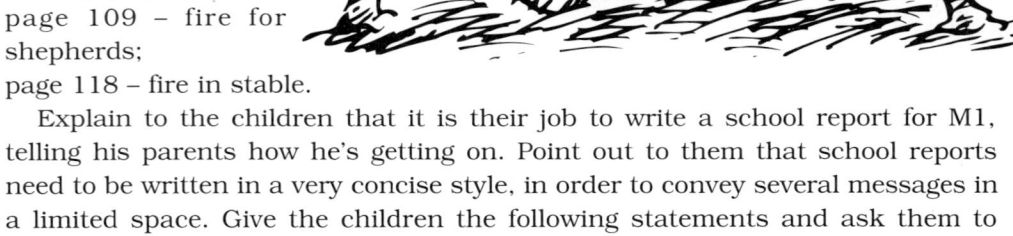

Explain to the children that it is their job to write a school report for M1, telling his parents how he's getting on. Point out to them that school reports need to be written in a very concise style, in order to convey several messages in a limited space. Give the children the following statements and ask them to suggest shorter alternative words or phrases:

1 M1 puts a lot of time and effort into his work. (*M1 is hardworking.*)
2 M1 has a strong interest in his work and is keen and eager. (*M1 is enthusiastic about his work.*)
3 M1 is always willing to do things for others and be of use when others need him. (*M1 is helpful.*)
4 M1 has good manners and is courteous to others. (*M1 is polite.*)
5 M1 gives his work his full attention. (*M1 concentrates well.*)
6 M1 always tries hard, attempting all work willingly, whether easy or difficult. (*M1 always makes an effort.*)

SCHOOL FOR DRAGONS — LITERACY HOUR UNITS

LESSON PLANS

GROUP WORK

Give each child a copy of photocopiable page 29, 'School report', which is a school report form. Talk to the children about writing an imaginary school report for M1. The children will put themselves in Mrs Jeffries' position and write a short report for each subject. Some subjects are covered in the book and the children can base their comments on these (for example Science – M1 has made a huge contribution to science lessons this term, using his fire to help us learn about heat/uses of fire/boiling water/testing temperature and what happens when paper is burned). Ask the less able children to write about these subjects first.

For subjects not covered in the book, the children can make up their own comments, imagining work that might have been covered and how M1 might have coped. The more able children should attempt to write a comment for all subjects. They may like to use a dragon theme to run through all the work, so for example in technology he could have made a model dragon, in history he could have studied the tales of Saint George and the Dragon, in music he could have listened to and played the song 'Puff the Magic Dragon', for RE he worked on the nativity play and in geography found out about Wales and the Welsh dragon!

Provide rough paper for the children to jot their ideas down and then tell them to write the finished version on the photocopiable sheet.

PLENARY

Ask the children to share some of their report comments with the class. Comment on those who managed to be brief, concise and to the point.

CHARACTERS IN THE BOOK

AFTER READING

RESOURCES

Poster, whiteboard or flip chart and appropriate pens, photocopiable page 30, writing materials.

WHOLE-CLASS WORK

We learn a great deal about the characters in the book, particularly Mr Wilkinson, Mrs Jeffries and M1, as we read through the story. The illustrations show us what they look like and the narrative and dialogue tell us what sort of animal/people/teachers they are.

During this session with the whole class focus on the character Mr Wilkinson, as a preparatory exercise for the work the children will go on to do in groups.

Using the extracts from the text on the poster, help the children build up a character profile of Mr Wilkinson. Read each extract aloud and ask the children to discuss what it tells us about him.

Talk to the children about adjectives: reminding them they are describing words. Read through the extracts about Mr Wilkinson on the poster again. Ask the children to suggest adjectives that describe him in each of the extracts and make a list of these together on the board. Then ask the children to add to the list any other adjectives they feel describe him, justifying their suggestion with an example from the story.

The list of adjectives to describe Mr Wilkinson in the extracts on the poster could include: proud; responsible; thoughtful/kind; understanding; funny/humorous; caring; confident.

GROUP WORK

Group the children into five, by ability, and encourage them to start by having a brief discussion about Mrs Jeffries and M1, talking about what they have learned

LESSON PLANS

about them in the story and giving reasons for their statements.

After their discussion, give each child a copy of photocopiable page 30, 'Character work – Mrs Jeffries and M1', and each group one of the four statements to work on. The most able groups should work on statements 1, 2 or 4 as these have the most pages to skim and scan, with the children working independently. The less able groups should work on statement 3 as it has fewer pages to skim and scan. These children could work in pairs to collect the information and then write their own sentences. Read through the sheet with them making sure they understand the task.

The children will need copies of the book to refer to specific pages. Advise them to skim and scan (explain this term) all the pages mentioned for their statement before writing their response which should be in their own words.

PLENARY

Ask one child from each group to share their character profile work with the rest of the class (five groups should provide five statements). Invite the children to add any other character information that wasn't mentioned. Draw the session to a close, concluding that we learn much about people (both real and fictional) by what they say and do and how they say and do it. Point out that other people learn much about us in the same way.

FIRE DRILL

RESOURCES NEEDED

Photocopiable page 31, writing materials.

WHOLE-CLASS WORK

Chapter 1 begins with Class 4J listening to a story when the fire bell goes. The children think it is only a fire drill but in fact there is a real fire. Read pages 5–8 to the children. Were the children in Mrs Jeffries class pleased when the firebell went?

Talk to the children about the last time the firebell went at your school. Was it for a fire drill or a real fire? Ask them what they have to do when they hear the fire bell. Confirm their suggestions by going over the official procedure that applies to your class or school. (Use the fire drill notice in or near the classroom to confirm the correct procedure.)

Talk to the children about procedural writing; writing instructions for carrying out procedures. Discuss how these must be in a numbered, logical order. Describe the formality of the language and presentation and the concise nature of such writing. You may like to give an example, such as the instructions for constructing a model:

1. Lay out the pieces.
2. Take cards A and B.
3. Slot A into B on the dotted lines.
4. Fold C in half.

GROUP WORK

Give the children photocopiable page 31, 'Fire! Fire!',

LESSON PLANS

which asks them to write instructions for a fire drill at school and then to consider whether some sentences are true or false. Remind the children to recall the discussion you have just had regarding the correct procedures for your school. Also remind them about the type of language used when writing instructions, explaining the terms 'clear' and 'concise' to them.

All groups should manage the first task independently. Less able children may benefit from help with reading and perhaps discussing together the true or false nature of the sentences in the second activity.

PLENARY

Invite some of the children to read through the fire drill procedures they have written. Ask if all the children agree, or whether somebody has a statement which nobody else has thought of. Go through the true/false sentences and discuss the children's responses.

AFTER READING

BOOK REVIEW
RESOURCES NEEDED
Photocopiable page 32, writing materials, rough paper.

WHOLE-CLASS WORK

Start a discussion with the children about book reviews. Remind them that review means to view again or look at again. Have the children ever read a review of a book which made them want to read it? Or which made them decide not to read something?

Gather general comments from the children about *School for Dragons* before asking specific questions focusing on the following:
* the general storyline;
* the different characters;
* the setting;
* the illustrations;
* the different events in the story;
* the humour.

Give the children three to five minutes to think about how they would recommend *School for Dragons* to someone who has not read the book. They need to think of a few sentences that will briefly summarize the story and persuade a friend to read the book. After three to five minutes ask for volunteers to address the class and make their recommendations.

GROUP WORK

Give each child a copy of photocopiable page 32 'Book review', and read through the questions with the children. Remind them that they need to write their responses in whole sentences. The less able children may need to organise a first draft of their responses on rough paper before writing their answers in neat on the photocopiable page.

PLENARY

Ask some of the children to share their book review comments with the class. Then have an open forum with general discussion about *School for Dragons*, reading stories in general, any other stories about dragons the children have read, the sorts of books the children enjoy most and any other related issues the children wish to discuss. Encourage the children to compare and contrast different books, giving reasons for their comments.

LITERACY HOUR UNITS — SCHOOL FOR DRAGONS

PHOTOCOPIABLE

Name _____   Date _____

DESCRIBING DRAGONS!

You have talked about dragons and about words to do with dragons.
✹ Using the notes you have made as a class, write a few sentences about each of the three words below to show the meaning of each word.

Mythical _____
_____
_____

Monster _____
_____
_____

Reptile _____
_____
_____

✹ Now use the information you have found out about these words to write four or five sentences explaining what a dragon is. Continue on the back. The first sentence has been started for you.

A dragon is... _____
_____
_____
_____
_____
_____
_____

SCHOOL FOR DRAGONS   LITERACY HOUR UNITS

PHOTOCOPIABLE

Name _____   Date _____

WHAT WILL HAPPEN?

✹ Look through the book at the chapter titles and illustrations. Use this list of chapter titles and write a few sentences saying what you think *might* happen in each chapter in the space. Don't worry if your story doesn't match up exactly with the story in the book!

Chapter 1	The Fire	
Chapter 2	M1	
Chapter 3	Reading	
Chapter 4	Problems	
Chapter 5	The Inspector	
Chapter 6	The Nativity Play	

✹ When you read through the story, remember to compare the predictions you made with what actually happens. How close were your predictions?

LITERACY HOUR UNITS — SCHOOL FOR DRAGONS

Name _____ Date _____

BRAINSTORM

You have been thinking and talking about words to do with fire.
✸ In your group, help each other to make four lists of fire words that describe what you might see, hear, smell and feel when you are near fire.

See...	Hear...	Smell...	Feel...

✸ Write some sentences about fire using the words in your list.

_____

_____

_____

✸ Read the following passage slowly and carefully. Choose an adjective or a verb to fill each gap so that the sentence makes sense. There are no right or wrong answers, but you can make the passage more interesting to read by using different words. If you can't think of a word to fill a gap, read on to the next gap and return to the one you couldn't fill a little later.

'Fire! Fire!'

The firebell went and we all had to go into the playground quickly and quietly. From the hut near the kitchen there were _____ clouds of smoke _____ into the sky. I could smell a _____ smell in the air. _____ flames were _____ the windows. Because of the _____ heat one of the windows _____ with a _____ bang and we all _____! It was noisy with the sounds of the fire _____ and the heat from the fire made us feel very _____. The firemen arrived and _____ the _____ building using _____ hoses and _____ of water. Soon the fire was out and we all cheered.

SCHOOL FOR DRAGONS — LITERACY HOUR UNITS

WRITING DIALOGUE

When we write dialogue we always:

- Use speech marks (inverted commas) for direct speech, the words that are actually spoken – "Hello", said Helen.
- Start a new line when a new person speaks – "Hello," said Helen. "Hello," replied Josh.
- Put commas, full stops, question marks or exclamation marks before the closing speech marks – "How are you?" asked Sophie.

✸ Read these sentences and then write them out again with speech marks and any other punctuation they need. The first one has been started for you.

1. the police will come and take him away answered lisa

"The _____

2. all right children lead on said mrs jeffries

_____

3. are you two going to play after school asked nelson

_____

4. what were you doing in the stockroom asked mrs jeffries gently

_____

5. we would love to read to you agreed the children

_____

✸ How did the characters speak? Fill the gaps using these words or choosing your own.

told   shouted   whispered   sobbed   chorused

"What do you think is going to happen to the dragon?" _____ Jessie.

"Put your chairs on the tables please," Mrs Jeffries _____ the children.

"Good afternoon, Mrs Jeffries," _____ the children.

"We've finished!" _____ Nelson.

"I didn't mean to start a fire," _____ the dragon.

LITERACY HOUR UNITS — SCHOOL FOR DRAGONS

PHOTOCOPIABLE

Name _____   Date _____

LET'S WRITE A PLAY!

You have read pages 47–55 as a scene from a play. Now you are going to write those pages as a playscript. Remember all the things you discussed in the class session! The scene has been started for you. Continue your play on the back of this sheet.

SCENE 3   *MRS JEFFRIES' CLASSROOM.*

Characters: Narrator, Mrs Jeffries, Lisa, Jessie, Nelson, M1 and Mr Dragon.

Narrator: Every day on the dot of four o'clock M1 turned up to be read to. But now the summer holidays were coming and neither Mrs Jeffries nor the children were sure what to do.

Mrs Jeffries: I think M1 should learn to read. I mean, we can't always be here to read to him. I think M1 should come to school.

Lisa: _____
_____

Nelson: What, *this* school?

Jessie: _____
_____

Mrs Jeffries: _____
_____

Narrator: _____

SCHOOL FOR DRAGONS — LITERACY HOUR UNITS

Name _____   Date _____

WHAT DO THESE WORDS MEAN?

✸ Read the three words or phrases next to each word below and circle the word or phrase that means the same as that word, when it is used in Chapter 4.

infectious (p56)   quickly affecting others   long lasting   an interest in insects

gingerly (p58)   clumsily   like a piece of ginger   very carefully

confess (p62)   shout loudly   say truthfully   admit to a crime

installed (p65)   placed in position for use   placed a person in a job   bought

bewildered (p69)   calm   happy   puzzled and confused

Each of these sentences below has a group of words that can be changed for one of these five words: **infectious, gingerly, confess, installed, bewildered**.
✸ Read each sentence and then write it again changing some words for one of the five words, making sure the meaning of the sentence stays the same.

She removed the dirt from the cut <u>very carefully</u>.
_____

The caretaker worked in the art area and <u>put in</u> a new sink and cupboard.
_____

He laughed so much that his laughter was <u>making everyone else laugh</u>.
_____

The little boy was <u>puzzled and confused</u> when the thunder and lightning started.
_____

My teacher <u>was very honest and said</u> that she did not know what the word meant either!
_____
_____

LITERACY HOUR UNITS   SCHOOL FOR DRAGONS

PHOTOCOPIABLE

Name _____   Date _____

THE DIARY OF M1

✻ Look at the list you made of what happened to M1 on his first day at school. Pretend you are helping M1 to write his diary for this day. It has already been started for you.

Day 1.

Got up and put on my school uniform. Mum said I looked really smart! When I got to school ...

_____
_____
_____
_____
_____
_____

✻ Now look at the list you made of what happened in the following weeks. Help M1 write his diary.

A few weeks later

_____
_____
_____
_____
_____
_____
_____

SCHOOL FOR DRAGONS   LITERACY HOUR UNITS

PHOTOCOPIABLE

Name _____   Date _____

FIRE POEM

✳ Read M1's poem again on page 89 of the book. Now write your own poem about fire with the same rhythm as M1's poem. Can you write more than one verse? Each verse must have four lines. The first two lines must rhyme and the last two lines must rhyme.

_____   _____
_____   _____
_____   _____
_____   _____

✳ Add -ing to these words. Remember to double the consonant or drop the 'e' if you have to. The first one has been done for you:

burn   burning   **drip** _____   **blaze** _____
whiz _____   **crackle** _____   **glow** _____
paddle _____   **scorch** _____   **hum** _____

✳ Choose three of these -ing words and use each one in a sentence:

1. _____
_____

2. _____
_____

3. _____
_____

LITERACY HOUR UNITS — 27 — SCHOOL FOR DRAGONS

SAINT GEORGE AND THE DRAGON

Many, many years ago there was a kingdom in the Eastern Mediterranean, called Silene. The king of Silene had a daughter, Cleolinda, who was so beautiful and sweet-natured that she was loved by everyone.

It happened that a huge, terrible dragon had made its home in the marshes to the west of the city. The Silenians knew it would not be too long before the dragon ran out of wild cattle to eat and it would then turn its attention to the city. They kept watchguards on the battlements night and day.

And then it came.

Roaring its defiance, the dragon flew right over the town, scorning the watchguards with their futile arrows. It seared the thatched roofs of the houses with fire and turned the city into an inferno.

The king immediately gave the order for two sheep to be put outside the city gates. The dragon saw the offerings, swooped down and bore them away.

Each day after this, the Silenians put out two sheep to keep the dragon contented. When they no longer had any sheep, they put out their goats, dogs, cats and – finally – chickens, until they had no livestock left.

With a heavy heart, the king ordered that the names of every man, woman and child in Silene – including the king himself and his household – should be put in a large urn. Each day a name would be drawn from the urn and that person would be tied outside the town as an offering to the dragon.

The bell in the castle chapel tolled mournfully next morning as everyone waited for the name of the first victim to be drawn. In stunned silence they heard the name:

"Cleolinda."

Everyone wept and wailed. The lottery must be taken again! They could not give their beautiful princess to that evil creature!

Cleolinda, however, was calm. "No," she said. "It is God's will that it should be thus. I will go freely, and I know he will send his angel to take care of me."

Since no one would take her, Cleolinda went to the dragon's lair by herself. She knelt down at the water's edge and began to pray. After a while, the water stirred and a dark, evil shape broke through the surface. Licking its lips, the dragon moved towards its prey with cold, unblinking eyes. Just as it was about to reach for Cleolinda, however, there was a great shout which echoed across the marsh.

"I know you! You are Evil. In the name of God I serve, I command you to leave this place!"

The dragon hissed and turned.

A white horse tossed its head and turned and pawed at the ground. Its rider was a knight, called George. He wore a helmet and chain mail tunic, a broadsword at his side, and he carried a tall lance. Both man and horse had an air of having fought many battles together.

The dragon screamed. Belching angry fire, it leapt into the air and dived towards the horse and rider. George levelled his lance and galloped forward to meet his foe. As the two came together though, the lance just glanced away from those impenetrable scales.

George came at the dragon again and again, using his shield to protect him from the dragon's breath, parrying those hideous talons. Then, just as the creature opened its mouth to flame once more, George thrust his lance down its throat. The dragon crashed to the ground.

George borrowed Cleolinda's long, leather belt and tied it round the dragon's neck. They travelled back into the city leading the dragon, and when they had reached the market place, George cut off its head with its sword.

Cleolinda's father gave George a very large reward for having destroyed the dragon, but George simply distributed the money to the Church and the poor.

Then he mounted his horse, bid farewell to the king and the princess Cleolinda, and rode away, never to be seen again.

Jackie Andrews

PHOTOCOPIABLE

SCHOOL REPORT

Merringham Junior School

TERM:	NAME:	CLASS:
Mathematics		
English *Speaking and Listening* *Reading* *Writing*		
Drama		
Science		
Technology		
History		
Geography		
Art		
Music		
PE		
RE		
General comments		
Signed		

PHOTOCOPIABLE

Name _____   Date _____

CHARACTER WORK – MRS JEFFRIES AND M1

✸ In your group, talk about Mrs Jeffries and M1 and discuss what sort of characters they are. Refer to the story if you wish.

Here are four statements, about Mrs Jeffries and M1, and some page references.
✸ Using the pages given, collect information which tells us more about each statement and why we know each statement is true.

1 Mrs Jeffries liked the children she taught. Pages 21, 22, 27, 28, 30, 42, 46, 90 and 108.	**2 Mrs Jeffries was kind to the dragon.** Pages 24, 25, 29, 30, 47, 48, 51, 54, 55 and 70.
3 M1 was sometimes sad, miserable, unhappy or ashamed! Pages 24, 27, 44 and 58.	**4 M1 was keen to read and became a very good reader.** Pages 29, 38, 45, 47, 48, 70 and 104.

SCHOOL FOR DRAGONS   LITERACY HOUR UNITS

Name _____   Date _____

FIRE! FIRE!

✸ Write out clear instructions for your class to follow when you hear the fire bell.

FIRE PROCEDURE

1. _____
   _____
2. _____
   _____
3. _____
   _____
4. _____
   _____
5. _____
   _____
6. _____
   _____

✸ Read the following sentences about what to do when you hear the fire bell. Some are true and some are false. Write true or false next to each sentence.

1. Tidy your work together and put it away. _____

2. Stay quiet and calm. _____

3. Run to get out of the building quickly. _____

4. Make sure your teacher knows if one of your friends is not in the class when the fire bell goes. _____

5. If you are changing from PE, finish changing before you leave the building. _____

6. You are safer if you face away from a fire. _____

LITERACY HOUR UNITS   SCHOOL FOR DRAGONS

PHOTOCOPIABLE

Name _____   Date _____

BOOK REVIEW

✱ Read all these questions and then answer each one, writing in complete sentences.

Did you think you were going to enjoy *School for Dragons* when you first saw the book? Why or why not? _____
_____
_____

What did you think of the story? _____
_____
_____

Describe the part of the story you liked best. _____
_____
_____

Which were the funniest bits of the story? _____
_____
_____

Which piece of work on the book did you like doing best and why? _____
_____
_____

If you could spend a day with MI where would you go and what would you like to do? _____
_____
_____

Look at the list of other Hippo stories at the front of the book. Write down three titles that you would like to read next. _____
_____
_____

SCHOOL FOR DRAGONS   LITERACY HOUR UNITS